FUN SCIENCE EXPERIMENTS

FUN SCIENCE EXPERIMENTS WITH COOKING

Claudia Martin

Illustrated by Annie Wilkins

WINDMILL BOOKS

Published in 2025 by Windmill Books,
an Imprint of Rosen Publishing
2544 Clinton St.
Buffalo, NY 14224

First published in Great Britain in 2022 by Wayland

Author: Claudia Martin
Illustrator: Annie Wilkinson
Series Designer: Rocket Design (East Anglia) Ltd

Cataloging-in-Publication Data

Names: Martin, Claudia, author. | Wilkinson, Annie, illustrator.
Title: Fun science experiments with cooking / by Claudia Martin, illustrated by Annie Wilkinson.
Description: Buffalo, New York : Windmill Books, 2025. | Series: Fun science experiments | Includes glossary and index.
Identifiers: ISBN 9781538396490 (pbk.) | ISBN 9781538396506 (library bound) | ISBN 9781538396513 (ebook)
Subjects: LCSH: Cooking--Experiments--Juvenile literature. | Food--Experiments--Juvenile literature. |
Science--Experiments--Juvenile literature.
Classification: LCC Q182.3 M37 2025 | DDC 507.8--dc23

Printed in the United States of America

CPSIA Compliance Information: Batch #CSWM25. For Further Information contact Rosen Publishing at 1-800-237-9932

Find us on

SAFETY PRECAUTIONS

We recommend adult supervision at all times while making the recipes in this book. Children should always be supervised when working with hot materials or knives. Always be aware that ingredients may contain nuts, seeds, eggs, yeast, or other allergens, so check the packaging for allergens if there is a risk of an allergic reaction. Anyone with a known allergy must avoid these.

* Wash your hands with soap and water before you start cooking.
* Tie back long hair.
* Rinse and dry all fruit thoroughly.
* Ask an adult for help with boiling, baking, or chopping.
* Check all ingredients for allergens.
* Clean up any spills right away.

CONTENTS

Give cooking science a try! ____ 4

Sugar crystal lollipops ____ 6

Color-changing noodles ____ 10

Fizzy lemonade ____ 14

Sourdough bread ____ 18

Invisible ink wraps ____ 22

Jiggling jelly ____ 26

Glossary ____ 30

Further reading ____ 31

Index ____ 32

Give cooking science a try!

Cooking is a great way to learn about science. The fun of cooking is experimenting and then examining the results using all our senses – and science is about exactly the same things!

Cooking involves lots of science. In the kitchen, we can explore the states of matter: solid, liquid, and gas. Solid foods, such as bread or cookies, need to be chewed or snapped. Liquids are the water, juice, or milk we drink. Gases are essential to cooking; it is a gas that fills our cake mixture with bubbles so it becomes fluffy in the oven.

The kitchen is a perfect place to explore mixtures and chemical reactions. A mixture is made when two or more ingredients, such as chocolate chips and cornflakes, are stirred together without being changed. A mixture can be separated into its parts. A chemical reaction takes place when two or more ingredients react to each other, making a permanent change.

When we bake a cake, chemical reactions change the ingredients forever. We can never separate the eggs or the flour from our baked cake. Instead, we can eat the delicious results!

STAY ! SAFE

The experiments in this book are not suitable for children aged under 7. Some of the equipment needed to carry out the experiments can be dangerous if not handled correctly. Please follow the instructions carefully and always ask an adult to help when the instructions tell you to. Please also follow the safety advice on page 2.

BECOME A SCIENTIST

Being good at science is not about knowing all the answers; it is about asking lots of questions. A scientist, whether aged 10 or 100, tries to think up possible answers. These possible answers are called hypotheses. They may be wrong answers, but they are interesting possibilities that help us learn more. A scientist then tests their hypothesis through experiments. Sometimes, even famous scientists realize their hypothesis was wrong, so they talk to other scientists and try again.

When trying the experiments in this book, work as a team so you can talk about your ideas. Try to predict the results of your experiments. Ask yourself what would happen if you did something differently. Record your results by writing, drawing, or taking a photo or video.

Sugar crystal lollipops

We are going to make lovely-to-lick lollipops using little more than sugar and water. We will use a technique called crystallization, which is a way of making a solid from a liquid.

You will need

To make 4 lollipops:

An adult to help you
8 ounces water
3 ½ cups white sugar
2 glass jars
Food coloring if wanted (two different colors)
Cotton string (choose string with a rough texture)
Scissors
Straws
Plates

1 ❗ You need to boil water for this step, so **ask for an adult's help**. If working in a classroom, this step could be done by an adult in advance. Bring 8 ounces of water to the boil, then stir in around 3–3 ½ cups of sugar, spoonful by spoonful. The sugar should dissolve, or seem to disappear, into the water. When no more sugar will dissolve, you have added enough. Leave your sugar liquid to cool for at least 20 minutes.

2 Pour your cool sugar liquid into two clean glass jars. Make sure there is at least 3 inches of liquid in each jar.

3 If you like, add a drop or two of food coloring to the liquid, using a different color for each jar.

4 For each team member, cut a piece of string about as long as the jars are tall. Tie the end of each string around a straw. Team members can share straws or use one each. When each straw is laid across the top of its jar, the strings should not touch the bottom or the sides.

5 Sprinkle the remaining sugar on a plate. Dip each string into the sugar liquid, then roll it on the plate so it is coated in sugar. Leave the strings to dry for around an hour.

6 Lay the straws over the tops of the jars, with the strings dangling in the sugar liquid. Leave for 3 to 5 days until your lollipops grow big. If the lollipops start to stick to each other or the jar, gently separate them.

7 Pour the sugar liquid out of the jars, then dangle your lollipops inside them again so they can dry. After around an hour, your lollipops will be ready to lick.

DO YOUR OWN THING

You could try creating multicolored lollipops! After a few days of growing your lollies, carefully move them to a jar containing a different colored sugar liquid.

What happened and why?

Crystals are solids with an ordered structure. Crystals can grow in nature, forming rubies and diamonds in the ground. We grew crystals of sugar, which are fun to eat!

Sugar is a solid. Each grain of sugar is made of many tiny sugar molecules. Molecules are groups of atoms, the building blocks for everything on Earth. The first step in our experiment was to dissolve sugar in water. When a solid dissolves, its molecules separate from each other and spread evenly through the liquid. This makes a mixture called a solution.

Our solution was supersaturated, which means that the water could not hold any more sugar molecules. Hot water is able to dissolve much more sugar than cold water, which is why we (or our adult) worked with boiling water.

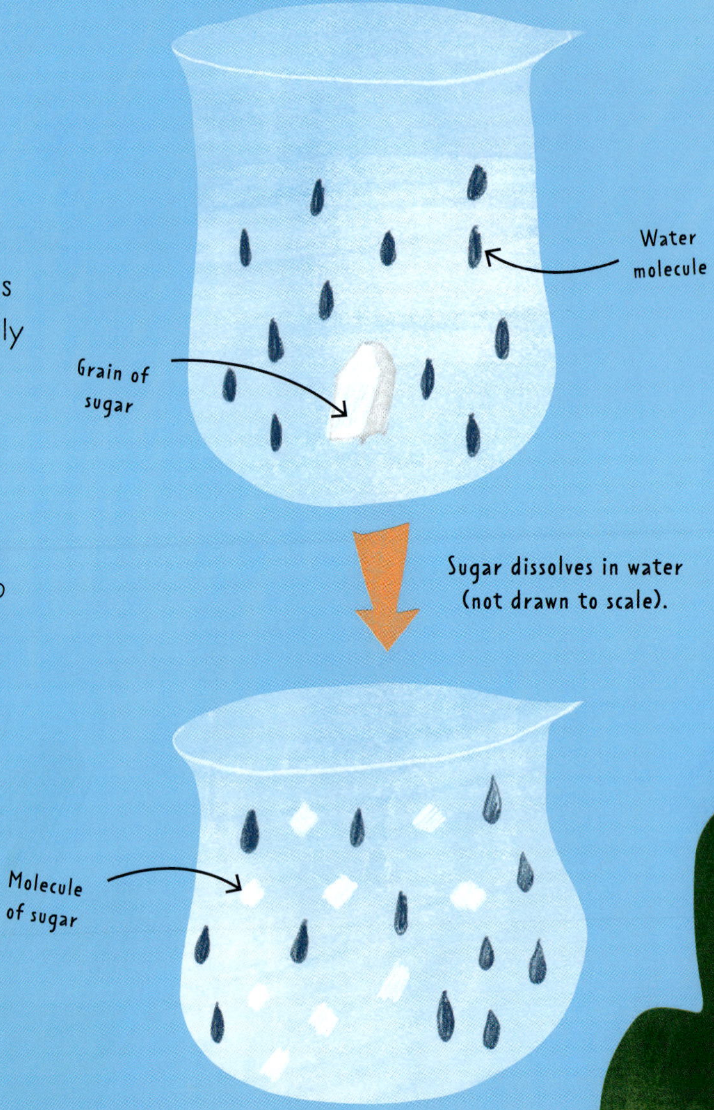

WHAT DO YOU THINK?

What might happen if we used salt instead of sugar for our experiment? (Apart from making lollipops that nobody wanted to eat!)

In a supersaturated sugar solution, the sugar molecules often bump into each other and start to stick together. When we rolled our strings in sugar, a few grains stuck to the string. These formed a base for other sugar molecules to stick to. More and more molecules stuck together around the string. They joined in an orderly pattern, repeating the same shapes. When a solid grows in an orderly shape, it is called a crystal. In nature, crystals often grow in solutions and in hot, melted rocks.

Under a microscope, we can see that sugar crystals grow in blocks and pyramids.

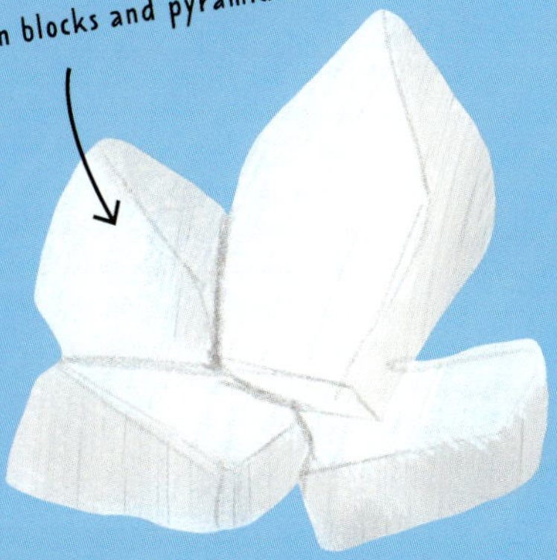

CRYSTALLIZATION IN ACTION

Crystallization is often used to help make medicines. The process starts when the ingredient for a medicine is dissolved in a liquid. By carefully controlling the crystallization process, crystals of the ingredient start to grow while impurities (or unwanted materials) stay dissolved in the liquid.

Color-changing noodles

These noodles seem to change color magically from purple to pink. This change is caused by a reaction between cabbage juice and lemon juice.

1 ❗ **Ask an adult** to cut the cabbage into quarters.

2 ❗ Place the cabbage quarters in a large saucepan and cover with water. **With an adult's help**, bring the water to the boil, then cook for around 10 minutes. Can you see any changes to the water in the pan?

3 ❗ Carefully, **with an adult's help**, add the noodles to the boiling water. Cook them for the time stated on the package, usually around 2–3 mins. For a deeper color, leave the noodles in the water for longer.

4 ❗ **Ask an adult** to drain the noodles into a strainer. Are the noodles the color you expected them to be? What were the other members of your team expecting?

You will need

To make 4 servings:

An adult to help you
7 ounces rice noodles
1 small purple cabbage
1 lemon
Water
Sharp knife
Large saucepan
Strainer

5 ❗ **Ask an adult** to slice the lemon into wedges.

6 Squeeze lemon juice onto half the noodles, either by dividing the noodles into two bowls or by dripping the juice in stripes and splashes. What happens when the lemon juice touches the noodles? Why do you think the lemon juice is causing a change?

7 Serve your noodles!

DO YOUR OWN THING

Try shaping your noodles to look like a rainbow. You could add some extra ingredients to complete the look, such as cauliflower for clouds and a fried egg for the sun.

What happened and why?

Purple cabbage gets its color from a natural chemical called anthocyanin. Anthocyanin reacts when it comes into contact with something acidic, such as lemon juice.

Many red or purple foods, such as purple cabbage, blueberries, and raspberries, contain anthocyanin. When we boiled our cabbage, it released anthocyanin into the water. The noodles soaked it up, making them purple too.

Most liquids are either acids or bases, even if only weakly. Acidic foods, such as lemon juice and vinegar, have a sour taste. Acids contain a lot of hydrogen ions. An ion is a type of atom or molecule that has a tiny electric charge. In contrast, bases have very few hydrogen ions. Foods that are bases, such as baking soda, taste bitter.

WHAT DO YOU THINK?

Can you think of some other ingredients that would make your purple noodles change color? What might happen if you added orange juice or baking soda?

! Liquids can be put on a scale from 0 to 14 depending on their acidity. This is called the pH ("power of hydrogen") scale. **Remember: Very strong acids and bases, like the acids in batteries and the bases in cleaning products, are extremely dangerous and must not be touched or eaten.**

Although we only experimented with an acid, anthocyanin reacts to substances that are either acids or bases; it turns pink in an acid and blue-green in a base. Adding lots of hydrogen ions makes anthocyanin look pink, while taking them away makes it look blue or green.

ACID INDICATORS IN ACTION

Substances that react to acids and bases are known as acid indicators or pH indicators. In laboratories, a commonly used pH indicator is litmus, which is made into paper that changes color in acids and bases. Litmus paper is often used to test a patient's pee for infections and illnesses, as these can change its acidity.

Fizzy Lemonade

We are going to add some fizz to a zingy lemon drink. To create bubbles, we will make a chemical reaction between lemon juice and baking soda.

You will need

To make 4 glasses:

- An adult to help you
- 20 ounces water
- 8 lemons
- 3 teaspoons baking soda
- 8 teaspoons sugar
- A spoon for each person
- Sharp knife
- Lemon juicer
- Jug
- Cups

1 ! **Ask an adult for help** with cutting each lemon in half. Working as a team, giving each person a turn, squeeze the lemons into a bowl to collect all their juice. If you have a lemon juicer, you will find it quicker and easier. Remove any pips.

2 Pour 20 ounces of water into a jug, then add the lemon juice.

3 Using a clean spoon for each person, allow every member of your team to sip your lemon and water mixture. How would you describe the taste?

4 Add 3 teaspoons of baking soda to the jug. What do you see and hear happening in the jug? What do you think has caused this change?

5 Add around 4 teaspoons of sugar until your lemonade is sweet enough to drink – but not too sweet!

6 Drink your fizzy lemonade right away. How does it taste? How does it feel in your mouth? Write down your team's observations.

DO YOUR OWN THING

To create your own fizzy cocktail, mix in other citrus juices. Stick with fruits that are highly acidic (see page 13), with a sour flavor. You could try oranges, limes, and grapefruits.

What happened and why?

Lemon juice is an acid while baking soda is a base (see pages 12–13). When acids and bases come into contact with each other, there is a chemical reaction.

When baking soda was added to your lemon juice and water, you saw and possibly even heard a chemical reaction take place. The mixture bubbled and fizzed. In a chemical reaction, an irreversible change (that cannot be changed back) takes place. Two or more materials react with each other, which changes the structure of their molecules. This creates new products and often brings about changes that we can see, feel, or taste.

WHAT DO YOU THINK?

What would happen if you waited for an hour before tasting your lemonade? Do you think it would still be fizzy?

When lemon juice (also known as citric acid) and baking soda (sodium bicarbonate) come into contact, they combine to create a new product: carbon dioxide gas. This is the same gas that is put into store-bought fizzy drinks like soda. When you tasted your lemonade, you could probably feel bubbles of carbon dioxide on your tongue.

ACID-BASE REACTIONS IN ACTION

Indigestion medicines often work with an acid-base reaction. These medicines help with problems like heartburn, which is a burning feeling in the chest caused by stomach acid.

The job of stomach acid is to break down food in the stomach. Sometimes, indigestion makes stomach acid rise up the esophagus, or food pipe, creating an unpleasant feeling.

Indigestion medicines contain a base. The base reacts with stomach acid, making it less acidic and also often creating a product: carbon dioxide. We feel, hear, and see the carbon dioxide as a burp!

Sourdough bread

To make sourdough bread, our first task is to capture and feed tiny microorganisms to make a sourdough starter. Then we will use the sourdough starter to bake a loaf of crisp and chewy bread to share!

You will need

For the starter:

5 ½ cups plain or bread flour

3 cups water

Tall glass jar

Spoon

Paper towel

Rubber band

For the bread:

An adult to help you

1 ½ cups sourdough starter (see Steps 1–4 below)

1 cup water

3 cups plain or bread flour

1 teaspoon salt

Large bowl

Spoon

Baking tray

! If you have a yeast allergy, do not try this experiment.

1. Put 1 cup of flour and ½ cup of water into a glass jar, then stir. Cover the top with paper towel then secure it with a rubber band. Place your jar somewhere warm but not in full sunlight.

2. After around 24 hours, stir your starter. Smell it and look for changes. Now spoon out around half your starter, putting it in the compost bin or trash. This will prevent your starter from getting too big! Finally, feed your starter by stirring in 1 cup of flour and ½ cup of water. Replace the paper towel.

3. Repeat Step 2 every day for 6 days. If you are working on it at school, someone will need to take the starter home for the weekend.

4. After around 6 feeds, your starter should be ready to use. If it is not bubbly and sweet smelling, continue feeding for a few more days. The best time to bake with your starter is when it is biggest a few hours after a feed.

5 In a large bowl, mix together 1 ½ cups of starter with 1 cup of water. Then stir in 3 cups of flour and 1 teaspoon of salt.

6 After washing your hands, knead (or push and pull) the dough for 10 minutes, then shape it into a ball. Put the ball back in the bowl, then cover. Leave for a day, placing the bowl in the fridge overnight.

7 ! **Ask an adult** to preheat the oven to 450°F (410°F for convection ovens). Place the dough on a baking tray, then bake for 35–40 minutes until golden brown.

8 Leave your loaf to cool before serving. How would you describe your bread's texture, taste, and smell?

DO YOUR OWN THING

You could add some extra ingredients to your sourdough loaf. Try adding 1 tablespoon of clear honey for a sweeter taste. For more texture, mix in a handful of chopped olives or dried fruit.

What happened and why?

Microorganisms called bacteria and yeast made your sourdough starter bubbly because of a process called fermentation. The starter filled your bread with bubbles, making it rise.

Bacteria, yeast, and other microorganisms are in the air, on your hands, and in flour. Microorganisms fed on the warm, wet flour in your sourdough starter, then started to multiply. *Lactobacilli* bacteria fed on sugar in the flour, changing it to lactic and acetic acids. This acid gave your sourdough bread its sour flavor.

The acid also killed off other microorganisms that might not be as safe to eat. However, yeasts in the starter were not killed. They also fed on sugar, then released ethanol and carbon dioxide gas. It was this gas that made the starter bubbly and later made your bread rise.

WHAT DO YOU THINK?

What would have happened if we had not left the sourdough starter to ferment for so long? Would our bread have tasted or looked different?

Fermentation is the process of using microorganisms to break down sugar, turning it into acid, ethanol, and carbon dioxide. Fermentation is often used to preserve foods, such as vegetables, by killing off harmful microorganisms. It also makes them taste sour. Your sourdough starter could last for years if you continued feeding it!

FERMENTATION IN ACTION

Fermentation can produce biofuel, which is a fuel made from plants or animal waste. Bacteria and yeast are used to break down the sugar in a plant like sugarcane. As they do so, they produce ethanol. This liquid can be burned in a car's engine instead of gasoline, to make heat to power the engine, which turns the wheels.

Invisible ink wraps

Let's make invisible ink, then use it to draw pictures on some tasty wraps. The pictures will not be visible until we put the wraps in the oven, when a chemical reaction will take place.

You will need

To make 6 pies to share:

An adult to help you
16 ounce ready-to-roll pizza dough
1/2 jar of jam
2 tablespoons sugar
1 teaspoon baking soda
3 teaspoons water
Rolling pin
Table knife
Jug or cup
Cotton swab
Baking trays

If you have a yeast allergy, do not try this experiment.

1 Roll out your pizza dough until it is around .25 inch thick.

2 Using a table knife, cut 6 rectangles of dough measuring around 4 inches by 8 inches.

3 Put 1–2 teaspoons of jam onto each rectangle, avoiding the edges. Fold each rectangle in the middle, then seal the edges of your square by folding and pressing them, so the jam does not leak out.

4 To make your invisible ink, put 2 tablespoons of sugar in a jug or cup. Mix in 1 teaspoon of baking soda. Then add up to 3 teaspoons of water to form a paste. Make sure your paste is not so runny that it will drip when you paint with it.

5 Dip a cotton swab in the invisible ink, then draw a pattern on the top of your wrap. Try a simple flower or star. Can you see the pattern you have drawn?

6 ! **Ask an adult** to preheat the oven to 425°F (400°F for a convection oven). Place the wraps on baking trays, then cook for around 8 minutes, or until your patterns are visible and the rest of the dough is pale gold.

7 Leave your wraps to cool completely because the jam will be very hot. What do you think made the patterns visible? Discuss your ideas with your team.

DO YOUR OWN THING

Instead of drawing flowers and stars on your wraps, you could write a secret message. For the best results, keep your message short and simple.

What happened and why?

In the oven, the heat caused a chemical reaction in the sugar solution, helped by the baking soda in the ink mix. It turned brown in a process that cooks call caramelization.

First of all, we dissolved sugar and baking soda in water to create a solution (see page 8). This liquid mixture was easy to write with. The solution was colorless, so our writing was invisible.

When the sugar was heated in the oven, its molecules started to break down into their separate parts. Some tiny particles called electrons were lost from the atoms. The molecules then started to reform, sticking together into long chains that have a darker color. This is caramelization. The baking soda sped up the process.

WHAT DO YOU THINK?

On pages 14–17, we learned that bases and acids react to each other. Can you design an invisible ink experiment (writing on paper rather than dough) using a chemical reaction between a base, such as a solution of baking soda, and a fruit acid, such as grape juice?

Oxidation is the scientific name for a chemical reaction that makes electrons move around. Oxidation is the reaction that turns an apple brown once it is cut open, because the apple reacts with the oxygen in air. It also makes iron rusty when the metal reacts to oxygen and water in the air.

CARAMELIZATION IN ACTION

When a few spoonfuls of sugar are heated slowly in a saucepan to about 340°F, they turn to caramel. As the sugar molecules reform as long chains, the consistency becomes sticky. The new molecules have different flavors from sugar, making the caramel taste nutty or buttery. The color turns dark orange.

Jiggling jelly

In this experiment, we are going to turn a liquid into a gel: a wibbling wobbling jelly! A gel is a semisolid with properties between a rigid solid and a pourable liquid.

You will need

For 1 tall glass of jelly:

- An adult to help you
- 2 teaspoons vegetarian gelling powder
- 4 teaspoons orange drink, like SunnyD, Tang, or Crystal Light
- 10 ounces water
- Handful of raisins
- 1 large, tall glass
- Saucepan
- Spoon
- Stopwatch
- Pencil and paper

Watch out for allergens in gelling powder. If you prefer, you can use powdered gelatin for this experiment.

1. Pour 4 teaspoons of orange drink into a tall glass. Add 3 ounces of cold water. Put the glass to one side.

2. Pour 7 ounces of cold water into a saucepan. Sprinkle over 2 teaspoons of vegetarian gelling powder. Depending on the brand of gelling powder, you may need to change this quantity. You need at least enough powder to set 10 ounces of liquid, but we have put in a bit extra so the experiment works fast! Stir until the gelling powder has spread evenly through the water.

3. **Ask an adult to do this step for you!** Heat the saucepan until the gelling powder solution is just starting to boil.

4 **Ask an adult to do this step for you!** Pour the gelling powder solution into the glass containing the orange drink. Stir for a few seconds to combine the two mixtures.

5 **Your solution will still be quite hot, so be careful!** We are going to test the viscosity of our solution right away. Viscosity is a measure of how easily a liquid flows. Thick liquids, like ketchup, have higher viscosity than thin liquids, like water. Carefully and gently drop a raisin from the top of the glass. Using your stopwatch, make a note of how many seconds it takes the raisin to reach the bottom of the glass.

6 Wait 1 minute, then time how long it takes another raisin to fall through the solution.

7 If you keep dropping raisins into your solution every minute, do you think the raisins will fall more quickly or more slowly? What will happen to the raisins eventually? Test out your predictions by dropping and timing raisins. Were your predictions correct?

DO YOUR OWN THING

Instead of raisins, you could drop berries or chocolate pieces. If you use a mixture of fruit and chocolate, do they fall at different speeds?

What happened and why?

As your jelly started to set, it became more and more viscous, so the raisins took longer to fall. Eventually, your jelly behaved like a solid, so your last raisin stayed at its surface.

Jelly is a fun mixture of solid and liquid; it has a definite shape but is also wobbly. Jelly has a definite shape because some of its molecules have formed links with each other, stopping the liquid water from flowing. A key ingredient in many vegetarian gelling powders is carrageenan, made from seaweed. It contains long, curling molecules. Once the gelling powder was spread evenly through the water, we heated it. This made those long molecules start to wrap around each other.

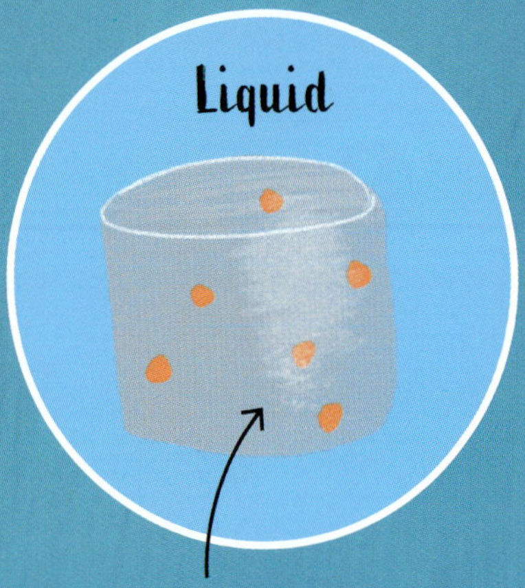

In a liquid, the molecules are not joined, so a liquid can flow.

In a gel, some of the molecules have linked with each other.

In a solid, the molecules are joined in a rigid pattern.

WHAT DO YOU THINK?

What do you think would happen if you asked an adult to put your cooled jelly in a saucepan and heat it up? Would the jelly become liquid again?

As the solution cooled, the string-like molecules of carrageenan started to bond to each other. This slowed the speed at which the raisins fell through the glass. The liquid was becoming more and more viscous because the molecules could no longer flow past each other. Eventually, the carrageenan molecules formed a three-dimensional structure, creating a semisolid gel and totally stopping the raisins from falling through.

GELLING IN ACTION

Scientists are experimenting with extra-strong gels in the shape of bottles. In the future, these could be used to hold drinks. The gel bottle could be eaten or left to decompose harmlessly. This would cut down the use of plastic bottles, which are expensive to recycle and often create litter.

Glossary

acid a substance that contains lots of hydrogen ions

atom the smallest portion of anything that can exist on its own; atoms contain smaller particles called protons, neutrons, and electrons

base the chemical opposite to an acid

carbon dioxide a gas that is found in the air

chemical reaction when two or more substances react to each other, creating a permanent change

crystal a solid with an ordered structure

crystallization forming a crystal

dissolve when a solid breaks up and mixes with a liquid

electron a particle found inside atoms that has a tiny electric charge

ethanol a liquid that can be used as fuel

fermentation the process of using microorganisms to break down sugar, often used to preserve foods

gas a substance that has no fixed shape or volume, so it will expand to fill any container

gel a semisolid that is mostly liquid but behaves likes a solid due to a mesh of linked molecules

hydrogen the simplest and lightest element (or type of atom) in the universe

hypothesis a suggested explanation for something

ion an atom or group of atoms with an electric charge

irreversible cannot be changed back

knead to stretch and squeeze with the hands

liquid a substance that flows but has a fixed volume (takes up a certain amount of space)

microorganism a tiny, simple living thing

molecule a group of atoms that are bonded together

neutral neither an acid nor a base

preserve to prevent food from rotting

rigid unable to bend or change shape

solid a substance that has a fixed shape

solution a liquid mixture

supersaturated when a solution contains as much dissolved solid as it can hold

viscosity a measure of how easily a liquid flows; more viscous liquids are thick and flow slowly

Further reading

BOOKS

Awesome Matter and Materials (Extreme Science),
Rob Colson and Jon Richards (Gareth Stevens, 2024)

Making with States of Matter (Science Makers),
Anna Claybourne (Wayland, 2019)

States of Matter (Science in a Flash),
Georgia Amson-Bradshaw (Gareth Stevens, 2018)

WEBSITES

Find out more about cooking and chemical reactions on these websites:

https://kids.britannica.com/students/article/chemical-reaction/623708

https://sciencing.com/chemical-reactions-involved-baking-cake-7173041.html

www.bbcgoodfood.com/recipes/collection/kids-cooking-recipes

www.stem.org.uk/elibrary/resource/30149

Index

acid (or pH) indicators 10–13
acids 10–13, 14–17, 20, 24
anthocyanin 12
atoms 8, 12, 24, 28

bacteria 20
baking soda 12, 14–17, 22–25
bases 12–13, 14–17, 24
biofuel 21

cabbage 10–13
caramelization 22–25
carbon dioxide 14–17, 18–21
chemical reactions 4, 14–17, 22–25
crystallization 6–9
crystals 8

dissolving 6, 8, 22, 24, 26

fermentation 18–21
flour 18–21

gases 4, 14–17
gels 26–29

hypotheses 5

indigestion medicines 17

jam 22–23
jelly 26–29

lemonade 14–17
lemon juice 10–13, 14–17
liquids 4, 6–9, 26–29
litmus paper 13

medicines 9, 17
microorganisms 18–21
mixtures 4, 8, 24
molecules 8, 9, 12, 16, 24, 25, 28

noodles 10–13

oxidation 25

pH (power of hydrogen) scale 12–13
predicting results 5

recording results 5
rusting 25

semisolids 26–29
solids 4, 6–9, 26–29
solutions 6–9, 22–25, 26, 29
sourdough bread 18–21
states of matter 4, 6–9, 26–29
stomach acid 17
sugar 6–9, 22–25
sugarcane 21

viscosity 26–29

yeast 20